Trailer Park Troubadour

Trailer Park Troubadour

By Justin Booth

Copyright @2013 D. Justin Booth

All rights reserved. Except for short passages for porposes of review, no part of this book may be reproduced in any form or by any other means, electronic or mechanical, including photocopying, recording, or by any information storage and retrieval system, without permission in writing from the author.

For my mother who has never stopped loving me, and I have been plenty damned unlovable at times. For Marcia Camp who has given herself and her knowledge and wisdom freely, and for Scott Welch for never firing me more than two or three times a day even if I don't get to your stuff because I am writing.

Table of Contents

Old Age is Carrion

Cowboys

Again

you get all kinds

Forbidden Fruit

I Never Wonder

The Jewel of the Trailer Park

The Tattoo

When We Are Rock Stars

Hot

joella turned tricks

crazy deb needs a new pair of shoes

like a little girl

Baby's Song

A Certain Kind

Like A Jim Croce Song

Sleeping Girl

Non Omnis Moriar

This One Thing I Pray

The Franzia Correlation

They Sicken

A Decent Poem

Love Poem You Shouldn't Write

I Told Her I Loved Her

The Bar

A Broken Hearted Life

90 Days Away

Old Age is Carrion

Should have died young

like James Dean

or Jesus.

The coolest ones

die for the masses

sacrifice self for mob love.

O.D. watching

co-dependant, white pantied

cuties wrestle in the Jungle Room.

The shock value

of teen rebellion

followed by a lifetime of

anti-establishment; fistfights, and felonies-

fashionable leather jackets,

black T's,

flashfire love affairs,

girls barely legal,

women shockingly mature,

tattoos and

avant- garde attitudes

on art, and literature, and fornication.

Wasted.

Should have died

in a motorbike wreck,

Martyred Hep Cat

like Jesus or Elvis.

Cowboys

I went to
A gunfighters
Funeral today

Not a

Cowboy hat

In sight

The glamour

Of toting

Pistols

Not quite

The same

Without them

The sad faces

And souls of

The men though

The same now

As a century

And a half ago

The guilt maybe

Or the things

They have seen

Again

And just as the sun begins,

in frozen yogurt hues,

the third hand car with its

grinding clutch and

its squeaking brakes

rounds the corner

creeping guiltily home

and she is relieved that

he is not dead

or locked up in jail.

She stands in the open

doorway hurt and angry and

scared that he'll never

quit binging and grow up

to be a father to the boy.

That the next may be the last.

She slams the door shut.

This is it then, he thinks,

she will leave me. This is the

last time, I swear it.

One last chance.

He is sorry

again.

You're so special? You're sad!
You can't stand to be with me?
I see it coming you know...
I am not stupid, just because
I don't say....

Tortured soul artist? So...
special? You hurt us-
you hurt me. Nobody even reads that
shit but me.
Come to bed, I love you.

And so it goes, a hundred,
maybe a thousand times more-
and it will be this
one day
that makes him sad.

you get all kinds

sitting in a

rock & roll

chicken shack

on a sunday

afternoon

when

the last mullet

in america walks in

wearing a fat redneck

underneath

who in turn

is sporting a

hunt often T

and a freightliner

ball cap

greasy

from the mullet

when the liquor

store

closes in the

bible belt states

you

get all kinds

Forbidden Fruit

Eden was wonderful.
At first glance,
I only wanted to know
her, eternally.
She seemed careworn,
distracted, enveloped
by hurts past.

Her hair, dark and short,
framed her face
in a way that made her
goth black eyes huge.

She showed me her
paintings, and I knew
she felt deeply.
In bed, after,
she was all knees
and elbows and
my side of the bed
like a child who
has had bad dreams.
I loved her, but
she needed the pain.

I never wonder

Why you love me.
You are so filled
with affection you
cannot contain the magic.

Instead I wonder
why you stay.

Why you stay
and listen to my
excuses for losing
another job, and
tell me things will
be better soon

Why you sit quietly
and listen to me
as I drink and
become more brilliant
by the minute
until finally
I am just an ass
who pisses in
the closet not

knowing where
I am.

Why you would
scrap together the
last few dollars
to get me a bottle
even though you
never had a drink
in your life and
could use a new brassiere
because the old one
is worn out and
it's the only one
you've got.

I often wonder at
night after you have
drifted off why it is
that you stay
with a mean old
bastard who
calls himself a poet,
based on the pile
of rejection slips
stacked up

like some great
paper mountain
waiting to be scaled
by only
the bravest souls.

Why, I wonder
do you weep sometimes
when I read my words
aloud to you,
when you are so
tough on the rest
of the world
a lioness with
bared teeth
at the ready

I never wonder
why I keep on loving you

forever,

though I don't
deserve to.

The Jewel of the Trailer Park

I would see her

out the kitchen window

of the rent by the week
trailer that I stayed in.

Made tired by the world,
stirring about
in a pale blue sun dress
frayed at the hem.
Chasing after a toddler
with the same
stringy blonde hair
and dirty bare feet.

She was the jewel of the park;

sometimes her laughter
like sleigh bells
would penetrate my mood.

When I cooked out,
weenies or burgers
on the grill,
the dogs who seemed to belong
to everyone or no one at all,
would wait and beg
and I would throw
them chunks of cheap,
red # something dyed
hot dogs

and the little jewel next door
would stand smiling,
staring out
the front storm door,

face pushed up
next to glass,
hand prints
and nose prints
and breath fogging.

I would wait
and hope her mother
would
come outside
so I could offer
her a beer.

Sometimes she came out,
but she never took
the beer, instead
she would go into my place

and slice tomatoes
and talk about
her daughter,
or the dogs or ask,
again,
what I was always
writing in the notebooks
I left scattered about.

The three of us
eating burgers and laughing,
a sort of white trash cover
from Saturday Evening Post,
until finally
they would go back home
and I would be drunk,
and she would be tired and

the little jewel would go laughing to bed.

The Tattoo

The tattoo

that I got

long ago,

faded now,

I can still feel

the scarring

of it's design.

The colors

dim

edges blurred

hardly

do I remember

why

I felt

compelled

to announce

to anyone

who saw me

shirtless

that you

were

mine forever.

Fat throwback

Sailor Jerry
letters pricked
into skin.
I touch it
tracing the path
of late night
artist's
staccato hand
thinking back
to your smiling
freckled face.
Eighteen
fresh from home
full of
expectation
and rebellion
ready to prove
yourself and
trust me.
You are long gone
now, but the
scar, and memory
remain, linger
as dust motes
float upward

in sunbeams

slashing a

motel comforter

and a yellowed

photograph of

that other time

when we were us

and two kids

walked

arm in arm

in sidewalk's

neon glow

ready

to take on

the world.

WHEN WE ARE ROCK STARS

i have a friend

a respectable women

a good wife and mother

who lives in a bastion

of knowledge and wealth

she is kind

of heart and deed

sometimes she comes to see me

AND WE LIVE

LIKE ROCK STARS

there is no limit to our decadence

we eat the richest deserts first then

dinner with heavy sauces

of dairy and drippings

DRINKING WINE

from the bottle without wiping

it's near escape

down our chins

WE SCREW

with reckless abandon

committing unnatural acts

in elevators of hotels

where we are not even guests

we drive to delta riverboats at three a.m.

and play blackjack and craps

I SHAKE DICE and

SHE BLOWS

on them making points the hard way

AND WE DANCE

early or late in clubs with pulsing music
too loud to stand

still

AND WE DANCE ALONE

skin touching skin with no music at all

save what is in our hearts

and then after

THE FINAL CURTAIN

we are ourselves again

the home maker and the hobo

until the next time

WE ARE ROCK STARS

Hot

It was one of those Motels
that stayed in business as
a shadow of its former self,
with weekly rates and
dope deals, and a pool
that always sat dry.
The faceless, open coil
air conditioners would
freeze up, and blow hot,
if you dared try them
before it was dark.
If you wanted a phone
it was five more bucks.
The girls never got phones,
so they would run
back and forth to my room
calling tricks or dealers
or sometimes their kids
they left back home.
I would sit on the landing
in a near crippled chair
hoping a breeze would
come there and see me .

The neighbour

came first

and I nodded

as he lit up a smoke.

He talked too much,

and used the girls,

and had a

crappy green tattoo

of Jesus or Willie.

I never liked him but

it was hot and you can't

open the windows

in those places.

joella turned tricks

before I met her

and only

sometimes after

like when she was

mad at me or

maybe herself.

we did dope together

at first but

eventually just drank,

such was our love.

her mother died

to soon, and

father was a monster.

he used her.

and his friends.

finally he set her

on fire with zippo

lighter fluid and

scarred her outside too.

we were hurt;

her as a child

me, less so, by

life and a bad

first marriage
we clung
to each other
like a cobweb
to an out of reach
corner,
such was our love.
we told each
other secrets,
drunk late at night,
sharing tears,
and fears
and passions.
A fiery sunset
beautiful but
for a moment
then gone,

such was our love.

like a little girl

the ghost of us

is the only thing

older than the

red and yellow

thai take-out

containers

spilling over

and around

the garbage can

with its living line

of ants

that separate

living room from

kitchen

the stereo

that i found

on the side

of the road

in sherwood

plays a

van morrison cover

and even though

your eyes were blue

it seems

dead on

the drink

in my hand

gone

and the ice

too far away

so i pour

straight from

the bottle

and sink farther

into the past

drinking

alone

to be with you

crazy deb needs a new pair of shoes

crazy deb was

a prom queen

gone bad

and she stood

 and cried

and prayed

one day like

she had

learned in vacation

bible school

all that time

ago over

tuna sandwiches

 and red

kool aid

jesus what

she wouldnt do

for a hit of dope

but god didnt care

or the

tricks were scared

so she went

back to the

little room

where she stayed

and stared

on better days

at the

soiled curtains

and black greasy hand

stains

around the

doorknob door

and shadows

in the corners

and the pulls

on the drawers

unblinking

thinking of the

tattered carpet floor

and her scuffed soled

shoes by the bathroom

were tired and ready

to sleep

and they were

sick of getting high

and beating

down the street

or flying

near her ears

on her toe curled feet

so

they kicked back and settled

down

while the crazy prom queen

came unwound

Baby's Song

The banjo man's
jangled ragtime
kept Baby on
the stroll until
the freakiest tricks
and the ones
who cruised for
boys were all
that were left.
I would be
waiting in
torn boxers and
yellowed undershirt.
Rumpled pages and
empty beer cans
crowding for space
on the cigarette
burned coffee table.
Her dog,
a one eared gyp,
was asleep and
farting by the
front door.

Baby always
called me
White Boy,
and after she
would come in,
we would lay
side by side
talking in low voices
until seduced by
slumber, but
Banjo Man
would play for
my Baby girl,
and I would wake
in afternoon heat
with no one
but a half deaf
flatulent dog
for company.

A Certain Kind

In those days

he was
just
beginning to be
noticed,
and they
would come
to him,.

Often
a student from
the local university,
sometimes
a Muse,
occasionally
rarely,
a protege

and they
would
pretend to love
him
and he them.

Flash fire
hot and fast.

Sweat and bruises
and sweet juices.

Tender
trailing fingertips
dirty talk

but it was
the inevitable

break-up,

tears and
curses.
The self-loving
heart-ache
that he craved.

YOUR POEMS SUCK!

shouted the best
of them,
the ones who
knew how to cut

as he
painted them out
of pictures,
gave waitresses
the pet names
he'd always called
them.

And drunk
on the petty
drama
of the
broken hearted,
he'd wander
blindly down
dirty streets.

Tickle the lock
of the boarding house
door
and enter
the smothering
silence.

Addicted,

he'd say
to himself
and sit
at the keyboard
lit by shabby
single lamp
and peck away
at the night

again.

Like a Jim Croce Song

There are photographs
in the attic
of my mind.
Old black and whites
and some
in sepia tone.

They are moments
captured from
inky shadows,
memories of the
days when I was
a better man.

Now I am
somebody else.

There are pictures
in sticky page albums
but they exist
only in my dreams,

I have surrendered
the luxury of possessions
as delicate as these,
subject to curling
from the heat,
mildew on rain soaked
days spent moving

too tired to
sit still.

The attic of my mind
saves the happiest moments;
the birth of a child,

a wedding, potluck
lunches at Grandma's
house on Sunday
afternoons, snapshots of
young love
in a wooded park..

Nights alone I sit
and leaf though them
sometimes
trying to remember,
sometimes
trying to forget.

Sleeping Girl

Having yanked

down the mildewed
shower curtain
while
pissing blood
or Red Stripe

or whatever

and stumbling
back to a
half crumpled
pack of Kools

on her

side of the bed,
he began to
study her
sleeping face,
her other-worldly

beauty.

He stood wooden
just for
a moment,
and thought
that she was
the one he
had loved.

Having pissed,
and smoking
a Kool,

(he hated menthols)

he wondered
if he were
the only one
who sold out
and settled,

for Jamaican beer,
and shitty smokes,

and a lonely girl

he didn't know.

Non Omnis Moriar

Bury me beside gravel crossroads

tell Ol' Scratch I did him bad.
Bury me with pugilist dreams, yesterday's glory
bedtime stories with my children long ago
before life's trick.
Make my monument a chrome bar stool
split red vinyl seat.
Remember wandering soul: gypsy spirit,
the way I would have loved if only I had tried.
Gusting winds North, South, East,
winds of Wild West blowing
scraps of paper bursting with words,
the real me.
Surround my grave with untamed heart house wives,
other men's wives, secret crushes I never knew.
Johnny Cash eulogy on a come down Sunday morning.
Funny stories like Father's funeral
anecdotal evidence, never conquering the world
settling instead for a draw.
Let loose hillbilly howls, shoot guns into the air
and whiskey from the bottle,
someone dance naked 'round the fire but
don't tell Mother.
Pray to whatever god that you know
that I remain free of Hell or Valhalla.
Instead reaping whirlwinds, chasing horizons,
passing away as sunset.

This One Thing I Pray

Truly I am
enamoured,
the very
idea so
appealingly
romantic
and final.

Darkest comfort.

I make it
grander in
my imaginings,
the way
a saddened
life-worn wife
of a more
stable man
might believe
excitement
and passion
eternal rests
in a drunken
poet

some prick
studying medicine
and on constant
look out
for a better option
than a crying
girl on the
kitchen floor
can't
compare at
first

to a dark
artist yearning
to brush aside
reality
and cry too.

Who is to say
it is not
the better choice?
Higher than
the mundane
and exceedingly
superior
to the unyielding
despair
that is my lot.

I am just
so tired and
too lazy
to carry
through, how?

I am not
a baker as
Plath,
so undignified.

As if I still
had pride,
traded
again to be sure
she was aware
I suffered.

The Holy
have quenched
my thirst

with vinegar,
a young priest
twists the tails
of Jonathan, David
and flees
that my sin
will not
befoul his pleasure.
He is Gods man.

How then?

Fire arms
seem iffy
and poisons
old school,
fancy flight
from building
or bridge?
luck has not
been kind,
too easily
then a crippled
ugly on the
surface
as my heart
has lived.

Sure I would
kiss death
and gamble
that there was
nothing
but darkness to
follow
but I am
a man of little
ambition

and drive.
It is no business
but mine
to make that choice
but I would
rather it blossomed
a surprise
as a blue-headed weed

yet soon

and my prayer
each night
to a god I hate
is to take me
and give me

this one thing
relief.

They Sicken

"They sicken of the calm who know the storm."
                                Dorothy Parker

They sicken of the calm
who know the storm,
it holds no promise.

The calm is a
black hole sucking
life in.

The storm is Life,
twisting, screaming
and dancing near Death.

Once you have
counted coup on
codeine and car wrecks,

been shot at and missed
every good thing
seems mundane.

Reality stands no chance
when sharpened point imaginings
soar infinitely.

The coolest green grass
of contentment is no memory
compared to swimming
the crashing surf of melancholy.

Those who know the storm
cringe against days blinding rays
but are comforted at the breast
of darkest night.

The Franzia Correlation

Neon glow

accented smiles
and clever
talk of
writers and
soft serve
politics.

Barefoot Moscato
philosophers
telling me
about Travon
and I wonder
if all the
ones who still
have hope
and great asses
ever get
the news
anywhere but
Facebook.

One more
bourbon
followed by
one more
beer followed
by one more
heart felt
nod, to justice
and Mother Nature,
and equality
for all.

Finally she asks
to see my place,
and we stop
at the liqour store
on the corner.

I grab a
cardboard
container
of Franzia and
wonder if
the shitty wine
in the
throw-away
box
isn't some kind
of metaphor
for the love
I make.

A Decent Poem

My hair would be long
standing out long
in all directions.
Rolling Rock
bottles like dead
men at my feet.
She would be
cleaning, organising,
whirling in all
directions.
I'd be watching
the television
not listening,
thinking about
the things I wanted
to say eternal.
I want a house,
I want babies,
I want to make
a difference in
peoples lives,
she'd say.
I'd nod,
and scratch
and smoke a butt.
I just wanted
to write a
decent poem.

Love Poem You Shouldn't Write

For Valentines Day

Listen,

I am not saying
that you are

not great,

I mean
you are.
You tell me
you love me,

show me,

you work hard
at your job
come home
and cook.

I am
just saying'
that sometimes
I need
a little more-

for Christ's sake

turn a trick
or something.
Screw the
neighbour

then tell me

it didn't

mean a thing.
Shoot at me
when I
come home drunk
or at least
throw
my coffee cup

full

of boiling joe
at my face
while I ignore
you mornings,
caught up
in poems by

Raymond Carver.

I don't want
to hurt you
but I am an artist

and Holy Crap

I kind of have
a reputation.

I can't be
writing love poems
all the time.

I Told Her I Loved Her

For all
of my days-
in every
kind of
storm,
I will remember
the night I
said it
out loud.

Riding a
rocket of
a few more
than I should
Diamond Bear
beers from the
the cooler
and a cheerful
crowd for
my lines,

we stood on
a downtown
sidewalk
littered with
cigarette butts
and past hope
dreams.

She held me
in those
fucking
rain forest-
green eyes.

Rapt.

I do,
I do.
I really do
love you...

I don't
want you,

well I do

but I don't
expect
anything.

Hell, the
damn thing
works better
if you don't...

I just want
to write you
ten thousand
love poems.

She smiled
and that
was good
enough
for me.

The Bar

Gravel roads
hunker down
between
row crops
and drainage
ditches lined
with cattails
and Pabst Blue Ribbon
beer cans
rusty at the tops.

Strange birds
run like chore boy
bandits away
from their nests.

The Bar,
an old share-cropper
bungalow,
sits hunched over
from the weight
of the years
and the memories.

The patrons
work for someone else
or draw a check
and spend days
drinking dollar cans
of bootleg beer.

A hand written
sign reads
"No Pot Smokin
or sellin",
but it is

okay if you
do it out by
the truck.

Gallon glass
jars offer
pigs feet or
pickled eggs,
and some days
The Bar
smells of charred
meat
cooked on a grill
made from a
30 gallon drum.

A Broken Hearted Life

They

say you can
die

of a
broken
heart

she
said to me
once

but

I
am more
likely

to get
hit by a
car

We were
castaway people
from the

other side
of the
glass

she
had lived

a crumpled
dollar bill life
like

a tattoo
on downtowns
arm

her
kisses tasted
like

lipstick and
vodka

I
was thinking
about

a sober Chistmas
but
she just

shook
her head

She
had hardluck
blues

Quality
House liters
the only cure

When
I would
leave

her,
to walk the
eight blocks

to the liquor store

her
face would be grey
as a cypress barn

When

I would
come back from
day labor

mornings

with
the brown paper
package

her
eyes would light
up like

I
just got out
of prison

I
see her
still

a thousand faces

sad old ladies

giddy little girls

she
was the saddest

muse

she
died of a
broken heart

90 Days Away

i like

single batch bourbon
e chats
with carla
real paper books
in my hand
sizzling
fried catfish
bloody grilled steaks
cold beer
straight from the can

i like
black cowboy coffee
ice cream
with toffee
hookers who sing
to the night
i like
the torn paper mess
of home
christmas mornings
and later the drunk
family fight

i like
joints not blunts
but i will
smoke a bowl

i like
jazz on the ipod
and country
rock and soul

i like

sports bars
with big screens
pay per view fights

no cover
no neckties
no dance floor
in sight

i like
fresh laundered
bedsheets
npr specials
and jimmy
who lives
on the streets

i like
cocktail mixers
with new
southern writers

paintings
by picasso
and old
zippo lighters

i like
the kindness
of strangers
small town
church service
mason jar
jellies and jams

i like
girlfriends
on xanax

river market poets
and late night dennys
grand slams

I have lived and worked in Little Rock my whole life and thought I knew this place. Through his poetry, though, Booth has showed me the city I love in a whole different way, brand new. He is nothing less than one of the finest poets I've ever met in person. While he doesn't sound like Whitman or write like Whitman, Booth's poetry always gives me the same feeling I get when I read Whitman: the feeling that he pours his soul into the vessel of each poem, sloshes it around a bit, then pours it back out, leaving a bit of himself behind each time. Every poem, then, a sacrifice. Such power. Such image. Such a voice. Such old and thoughtful loveliness.~ David Koon, graduate of the Iowa Writer's Workshop, he has also taught film, literature and creative writing for 15 years.

Justin Booth writes about the places the heart sometimes wants to forget or ignore and in doing so he brings light to places where the reader can find tenderness and passion amongst the lost men and women of this unforgiving world. Such is redemption. Mark his words. He brings us into the fire and beyond.~ Brendan McCormack, author of Selling Heaven . He lives and writes in Dublin, Ireland.

Justin's writing is a mix of prose and poetry. Poetry in that words on the page flow and connect together like music notes. Prose in that you are there in the bar, the trailer park, the street - - wherever he is speaking of. His characters get inside your head and you are them for a moment, until you turn the page...and begin another poem.~ Laura Loughridge, President River Market Poets, Poets Roundtable of Arkansas.

He writes of life, love, gain, loss, all in the raw, all seen with an unsentimental eye and yet with a deep love of place and people. If I could choose three writers to go drinking with tonight he would be there with Kerouac and Bukowski. ~ Michael Corrigan is an Irish poet often featured in Elbow Lane Poetry, and the Femoy Poetry Festival.

Made in the USA
Lexington, KY
05 March 2014